TEAR ME WIDE OPEN

A BOOK OF EDGY POEMS

TARA SCHOOSE

iUniverse books may be ordered through booksellers or by contacting:

iUniverse
1663 Liberty Drive
Bloomington, IN 47403
www.iuniverse.com
844-349-9409

Because of the dynamic nature of the Internet, any web addresses or links contained in this book may have changed since publication and may no longer be valid. The views expressed in this work are solely those of the author and do not necessarily reflect the views of the publisher, and the publisher hereby disclaims any responsibility for them.

Any people depicted in stock imagery provided by Getty Images are models, and such images are being used for illustrative purposes only.
Certain stock imagery © Getty Images.

ISBN: 978-1-6632-2524-5 (sc)
ISBN: 978-1-6632-2526-9 (hc)
ISBN: 978-1-6632-2525-2 (e)

Library of Congress Control Number: 2021913146

Print information available on the last page.

iUniverse rev. date: 06/29/2021

TEAR ME WIDE OPEN

A BOOK OF EDGY POEMS

A journey through suffering to reach an expected end. One woman's
story of walking through the mud and becoming a lotus.

TARA SCHOOSE

DEDICATION

To all my children, and to all those who have loved too hard, loved the wrong people, or loved everyone but God and themselves. To those who feel as if they are not enough. To those who let the opinions of others cause conflict within them and distort their own perception of themselves. I invite you to hear what God says about you. Continue to rise, to crush your dreams, to be your most authentic selves, and to shine as you were meant to shine. God is the poet of the world and of everything in it. I wrote *Tear Me Wide Open* as a testimony that his words never come back void. I wrote this to bring awareness to the injustice and inequalities here in the United States. We face adversity in the realms of gender, creed, and ethnicity. We ask for swords from on high to destroy all that is wicked, for all darkness to be revealed and turned to light, and for the truth to be told.

A long, hard road of losses of love can really put life into perspective when, and only when, we listen to God and not our own egos.

TABLE OF CONTENTS

PREFACE

Tear Me Wide Open is a book of poems written by my ego, my flesh. True peace cannot live where there is any attachment to worldly outcomes. In these poems, you will read the story of my sufferings. The scriptures I have included are my true everlasting peace, the only things that stay the same forever. God is a constant, and our suffering is maximal without him. These are my experiences. Be warned: the ego is a bitch.

Scripture quotations are taken from the King James Version of the Holy Bible.

DEJECTION

We have no status;
It's dead and gone.
You liked my status with benefits, huh?
But, boy, check your census.
You're just a taker,
But you're playing with a mother of three,
A homemaker.
Sorry she made a mistake or two in thinking
That you'd be true to her.
But she can see it in your eyes—
Brown—
That you're full of it,
Nowhere near legit,
Grimy!
For the fuck of it,
Whom should I pass this dick to, though?
Nobody wants it if you ain't an asset.
Good pussy, then you bang it and trash it.
Plus,
You're an addict,
A facet.
You steadily wonder
Where you'll get your next nut.
You hired a prostitute once
Just to play with her butt.

"Lola's got the most beautiful butthole."
"How do you know that?"
She's somewhere in LA with her boo, though.
Somehow these bitches are way smarter than me,
But they still look at me as if I've got a disease.
I'm not a taker.
I might be naive,
But I am cared for by our Maker.
I don't think you are different from me,
But I will say that
I'm not the same type of bitch,
The type who schemes,
Just looking for some free shit.
And I'll break you off maybe once or twice,
But you can't make a ho a housewife.
God uses angels upon the earth
To teach us things
From the day of birth.
God bless the baby
Who was born crack-addicted to a lady
Who was very lit.
So hit this bong,
Not this glass dish
That has you tricked.

Who is a virtuous woman? For her price is far above rubies.

The heart of her husband doth safely trust in her.

So that he shall have no need of spoil.

She shall do him good and no evil all the days of her life.

She seeketh wool, and flax, and worketh willingly with her hands.

She is like the merchants' ships ; she bringeth food from afar.

She riseth also while it is yet night, and giveth meat to her household, and a portion to her maidens.

She considereth a field, and buyeth it; with the fruit of her hands she planteth a vineyard.

She girdeth her loins with strength, and strengthenest her arms.

She percieveth that her merchandise is good:

Her candle goeth out by night.

—Proverbs 31:10–18

PAWG

Haven't you heard the words some speak

In church

To a priest?

Don't tell your confessions.

Instead, take them as lessons.

To another human being, your blessings are dead.

Your faith was in humankind

Instead of the Godhead.

They are steadily tryna stain us with all that made us.

Chivalry is dead,

So give me some head

And I'll throw you a band.

Sleep well tonight.

May the stars shine bright.

He said, "Blink twice if you need some help."

But he doesn't even hear me when I yell,

"Fifteen dollars ain't much,

But to a blond crackhead,

It is just enough."

Ch-ch-ch-changin'.

Shit's getting major,

A favor for a favor.

That dick is what you gave to her.

It's the new revolution.

Ain't no tellin when they'll clear the pollution

And we'll start to see clearly

(Now the rain is gone).

You prey on thick, healthy bitches

Who can pay your rent

And get your teeth fixed.

I ain't no ho.

I've got hos.

Y'all the only muthafuckas

Willin' to sell yo souls,

But ya won't even share ya plate.

Once full of resentment,

She's healing now,

No longer the milk cow.

But that's not me.

There has to be a gray area.

I try to see

The middle

In the swinging

Of the pendulum.

See,

Looking for a center.

Like yoga.

But you're

Bogus.

You stay in the mud.

And I

Am the lotus.

She will outgrow you.

She's just gotta

Stay focused.

Trust in the Lord with all thine heart; lean not unto thine own understanding.

Proverbs 3:5

DV

Domestic violence.
Lower your voice.
Chase her out of the house.
Throw a shoe and mop water
All over your spouse.
Am I?
Will you take my last name
Or give yours to her?
I bet it just depends on the size of her purse.
Whose line is it anyway?
Whose house is it
Since I just paid the rent?
Rejection at its finest.
Gee, thanks.

IN GOD WE TRUST

It ain't my fault you fucked the whole team.
But you stay, keeping me creamed.
Yes,
Still searching
For the American.
She went from girl next door
To neighborhood ho.
XOXO.
So she changed for you.
Boo-boo.
My nana came straight from Italy,
WOP,
"Without papers."
But nobody made them stay behind,
Get in the grind.
They had a pizza kitchen with pasta of all kinds.
You're wondering what they were kneading.
Dough.
You say I'm entitled,
But what you don't know
Is that the struggle brought out
My hustle.
They fought for our freedom.
In God we trust.
And, yes, we all need him.
So get up outta the dust
And receive him.

VAMPIRE

Am I dreaming?

Ya must be deceivin'.

You know what I need when we be freaking,

But you only sometimes hit it on the weekend.

From the eight ball, yo breath start stinkin'.

You just take the microphone.

Hope you don't

Expect any dome.

You are just like

David the gnome,

Forever alone.

They don't call you Dolo for no-no.

Fool,

You will forever ride solo.

You act like an only child. Oh, you were one.

So you won't open doors and wine and dine this woman.

I wine and dine.

Don't you forget,

We're rare and very few in number.

You told me today the man of my dreams will only stay

In my dreams, those being his only remains.

You said that if I think I will find him,

I must be insane.

She couldn't be saved.

She went to rehab once,

But it was a waste, yeah.

You gotta want to get clean.

But how do you want to when your world is so small

That you can't see past your next bag

Or the next scheming type of bitch?

We're different.

I'm not all innocent,

But I see both sides.

You're blind in one eye.

I'm the one who decides

You've got an angel on one side.

But you can't escape your wicked mind,

The constant state of lack. Your daddy

Died of a heart attack.

That wasn't even enough to change ya.

But that's how God made ya.

A fava' for a fava'.

That dick is all she chased ya for.

Is that what you are,

A human-sized dick

Who rides around with the next fast chick?

She is done with being a broke ho.

Not your bank account;

It gets much deeper though.

She's talking about an attitude of lack,

Your fight-or-flight.

You stay up all night

Just to tell her in the morning to

Take flight.

Get out of the house!

For we wrestle not against the flesh and blood, but against principalities, against powers, against the rulers of the darkness of the world, against spiritual wickedness in high places.

—Ephesians 6:12

And I saw the woman drunken of the blood of the saints, and with the blood of the martyrs of Jesus: and when I saw her, I wondered with great admiration.

—Revelation 17:6

And they had hair as the hair of a woman, and their teeth were of the teeth of lions.

—Revelation 9:8

Only be sure that thou eat not the blood; for the blood is the life; with the flesh: and thou mayest not eateth the life with the flesh.

—Deuteronomy 12:23

PNEUMA

I even talk of suicide and dying.
I done been through it all,
Wanting to get rich
Or die tryin'.
But check it,
Life is a risk, carnal.
There is more to it than meets the eye.
Tryna catch the spirit,
The mortal dies.
But listen carefully;
You can hear it in the shade.

Sometimes snakes
Are the only remains.
Fake friends
Smile to your face and find their ends.
Let's go to a place
Where we no longer pretend
To be balanced.
But we trippin' one way or the other.
Will we be naked or covered?
You or another?
Chase that bag or recover?
I have tasted the bitter fruit.
Who would have thought I would fit this shoe?
Nike Cortez.
Coronavirus,
Another flu?
As we drift away into the sunrise,
Open your eyes.

It hurts too much sometimes to realize
I've been running from myself.
What have I got to lose?
The only thing that I came here with was abuse.
I've been fighting ever since
I was conceived in my mother's womb.
I state real facts,
Nothing topped off with sugar.
Cuz we all know when you sugarcoat the truth,
Somebody might get popped off.
Why'd they have to take the greatest?
Why sometimes are we worried too much about
Becoming famous?
That's the carnal shit that I don't like to speak of.
I spent too many years tryna
Dislocate my ego.

RIP,
B.I.G., Tupac, and Nipsey.

For they have shed the blood of saints and prophets, and thou hast given them blood to drink; for they are worthy.

—Revelation 16:6

There is a generation that curseth their father and doth not bless their mother There is a generation that is pure in their own eyes and is not washed from their filthiness. There is a generation oh how lofty are their eyes! And their eyelids are lifted up. There is a generation whose teeth are as swords, and their jaw teeth as knives, to devour the poor from off the earth and the needy from amongst men.

—Proverbs 30:11–14

And the Lord God formed man of the dust of the ground, and breathed into his nostrils, the breath of life; and man became a living soul.

—Genesis 2:7

ODIUM

It's not that she's weak;
It's just that you are a troll.
You cut into her deep.
It left a hole.
Emotions run deep.
You say I'm too emotional,
Blood in, blood out.
It's not a compromise,
Cuz water runs deep when you read between the
Lines.
I'm not perfect—I don't claim to be—
But you keep
Cutting,
Cutting,
Cutting into me.
You always hurt my feelings.
Guess you don't have any.

Your body is like a canvas

Of torn-up pussies.

But I was a fool.

I thought you were into me.

Instead you were looking for whatever you could get.

You always said

You couldn't miss what you couldn't hit.

Every end has its roots or its reasons for being.

Like, why did so many great ones have to die,

With so many others left wondering why?

So many lives,

And bribes caused compromise.

Like, why the fuck are we

Fucking with each other,

And why did you have to be raised by a junkie mother?

Oh, it's okay

If it's not heroin,

Rather cocaine.

He sits and contemplates,

Not breathing another day.

These things I have spoken unto you, that in me ye might have peace. In the world ye shall have tribulation; but be of good cheer; I have overcome the world.

—John 16:33

CLOWN

These hos stay ready to help me down,
But where are they when I fall?
Nowhere to be found.
Like a scared dog in a pound,
You left me.
And now you're not here when I am picking myself up off the ground.
What do I do now?
Stay up?

They sacrificed unto devils, not to God; to gods whom they knew not, to new gods that came newly up, whom your fathers feared not.

—Deuteronomy 32:17

Then certain philosophers of the Epicureans, and of the Stoicks, encountered him. And some said, "What will this babbler say?" Other some, He seemeth to be a setter forth of strange gods: because he preached to them Jesus, and the resurrection.

—Acts 17:18

For the preaching of the cross is to them that perish foolishness; but unto us which are saved it is the power of God.

—1 Corinthians 1:18

For he that wrought effectually in Peter to the apostleship of the circumcision, the same was mighty in me toward the Gentiles.

—Galatians 2:8

WATER

Today I choose to feel fluid like water.

Fuck the heaviness, guilt, shame, inadequacy. These are heavy, and I choose to see the light.

I am advancing more and more until you are but an inkling in my sight,

Bringing back the Holy Spirit like in the days of old,

When scraping by felt like less of a struggle.

I used to cry,

But now I'm a tough dude.

The constant struggle of being scared to be broke

Was the very thing that kept me held in a tight choke

Hold, not realizing that the bondage

Of this family

Was making me ill.

I went to three different therapists and popped like five different pills,

But something was missing.

It was more than on the surface;

I was burning rapidly

But appearing to be A-OK.

I listened to different teachings,

Everything except Jesus.

He is the only way, so leave the Jesus pieces.

Cuz it's not the cross.

Most of y'all are lost,

Looking down at a black man at Hobby Lobby:

"What's he doing here?"

He's supporting his wife

With her hopes and dreams.

You stare

With malice in your heart.

What God put together,

Let no human being take apart.

God says in his Book that whosoever believeth in him shall not perish but have everlasting life.

And his name is heard by these in times of darkness.

They are the light.

His children,

They walk in his law.

They feareth the Lord.

They are blessed,

Placed higher than the rest.

Instead he's a disgrace to the United States.

If we look not to the expansion you claim

Regarding the dollar

But instead to giving light and praise unto the Father …

You are not like him.

How can you claim to be?

You worship the dollar—

Easy to see

With the naked eye.

May the truth set you free,

GD.

For with God nothing shall be impossible.

—Luke 1:37

PLASTIC

You are plastic
Just like your smile—
Mean, then nice for a while.
Bipolar rage.
God! These kids in these cages
Killed hundreds of thousands.
Now we're steadily debating
Things about our country,
But these rights are being stripped and taken
From mostly minorities.
Cuz he's tryna shut down the USPS, which has
One of the highest
Numbers of minority employees in the country.
Oh, you're attacking
These communities?
He's siding with Russia
But fucking with the bread and butta
Of the young
Middle class
Among the darker races.
We see racist faces just telling us to go right or stay left, but what is right?
And what is left anyway?
They stain
Young black Americans.

Mostly in minority neighborhoods

The mail-in ballot is getting shut down.

Donald Trump was able to confess

That he supported Black Lives Matter and Antifa

With stimulus payments and unemployment checks.

He said he would be there at Capitol Hill to stand with his supporters.

He invited the Proud Boys to stand down

And stand by.

Now he pays officers and underage civilians,

Not to mention the two hundred thousand

Dead people on his head.

I can almost smell the lead:

One shot,

Two shots,

Three shots

Fired off

While he walks away.

But the only thing we're worried about are the organizations that fund the cops.

I'm not saying to riot;

You fell for the scheme.

I'm saying to look at who it is he's claiming to

Be anarchists.

But he creates confusion

Among the heathens

And has liaisons with other nations.

And treason is the only reason.

For I know the thoughts that I think of you saith the Lord, thoughts of peace and an expected end. Then shall ye call upon me, and ye shall go and pray unto me, and I will hearken unto you. And ye shall seek me and find me when you search for me with all of your heart.

—Jeremiah 29:11–13

TOY BOY

If she had nothing,

You would send her trucking.

See, you're missing more than just one thing.

She was hoping for a human being.

You are animalistic,

Primal,

Pitiless.

But I'm asking for you to be the change you seek in the world,

To stop yourself from taking advantage of this beautiful girl

Who wishes you no ill will at all.

Maybe she should look at you like the giant cock you are

And stop trying to build a life with a fuckboy.

She should have listened to those who told her

You would just toy with her emotions.

AFTERWORD

I had to get my spiritual growth and long-suffering out and onto paper. *Tear Me Wide Open* began when I was in a bad place. Having discovered grace and glory through God, I needed to share that with the world. I decided on an approach using edgy realism to attract others going through spiritual growth and also to uncover God's gifts!

GLOSSARY

dejection. A sad depressed state; low spirits.

domestic violence. Violent aggressive behavior within the home typically involving the violent abuse of a spouse or partner.

odium. General or widespread hatred or disgust directed toward someone as a result of his or her actions.

PAWG. Phat ass white girl.

pneuma. (In Stoic thought) The vital spirit, soul, or creation of a person.

vampire. A creature from folklore that subsists by feeding on the vital essence (generally in the form of blood) of the living. In European folklore, vampires were undead creatures that often visited loved ones and caused mischief or deaths in the neighborhoods they inhabited while they were alive. They were shrouds and were often described as bloated and of ruddy or a dark complexion, markedly different from today's gaunt, pale vampires, which is a type that dates from the early nineteenth century.

Printed in the United States
by Baker & Taylor Publisher Services